Praise for the Lessons Downton Abbey Book Series

Leadership Lessons From Downton Abbey

"This book is a great introduction to the world of leadership and management and offers a handy overview of key leadership principles and management strategies... I loved *Downton Abbey* so for me the book was a delight. It's practical and easy to read and makes sense of sometimes complex issues."

SaskBooks Reviews

"One of the things the book pulls nicely together after these four sections (leading yourself, leading employees, leading culture, leading with others) is what you refer to as effective leadership and the four critical areas — insight, self-discipline, courage and influence. Those things are transcendent whether we are in the earliest part of the 20th century or now in the earliest part of the 21st... It's a very interesting read."

John Gormley, Broadcaster, Lawyer, Author, Former Member of Parliament

Change Management Lessons From Downton Abbey

"Writers Jeanne Martinson and Laurelie Martinson have leveraged their interests in management, communications, leadership, and the popular British TV series *Downton Abbey* to inform business and organizational leaders.... There's much interesting material here, for both leaders and laypeople."

SaskBooks Reviews

"Very interesting new book... In Season Two, (Downton Abbey) gets its first telephone. That was an amazing time in the earliest part of the 20th century for managing change. So much of our current rapid technological change is simply finding new tools or techniques to do what we already do. This was completely a new paradigm altogether."

John Gormley, Broadcaster, Lawyer, Author, Former Member of Parliament

CHANGE MANAGEMENT LESSONS FROM
DOWNTON ABBEY

by
Jeanne Martinson
Laurelie Martinson

A WOOD DRAGON BOOK

This book has not been approved, licensed, or sponsored by any entity or person involved in creating or producing the television series, Downton Abbey.

Change Management Lessons From Downton Abbey
By Jeanne Martinson and Laurelie Martinson

Published by:
Wood Dragon Books
P.O. Box 429
Mossbank, Saskatchewan
Canada
SoH3Go

Telephone +1.306.591.7993
www.wooddragonbooks.com

Cataloguing and Publication Data available from
Library and Archives Canada

ISBN: 9781989078013

Inside and cover art by Laurelie Martinson

Dedication

To a generation of people who
implemented the greatest amount of change
in recorded history.
- From the wireless to cell phone
- From the telegram to email messages
- From the horse drawn buggy
to electric cars
- From the first aircraft flight
to space shuttles.

Of you
we are in awe
and to you
we are in debt.

Note from the Authors

As a professional who has spent more than 25 years consulting and leading, I have observed the ongoing challenge that organizations have implementing change and making that change succeed long-term. As explored in the first book of this series, *Leadership Lessons From Downton Abbey*, insights and practices from the past can be applied to solve problems in the present. Downton Abbey provides a wonderful analogy for discussing change management tools in a new way.

Laurelie Martinson

The idea for this book series came from a discussion about the many interesting leadership and management examples dramatized in the television series, *Downton Abbey*. The discussion grew and soon we were comparing the scenes in the drama set a century ago to workplace challenges of today.

It has been a pleasure to be able to combine my love of history with my passion for leadership in such a unique and enjoyable format.

Jeanne Martinson

Caveats

Scenes described in the following chapters may not appear in the order portrayed in the television series, *Downton Abbey*. Only the characters explored in this book are identified in the organizational charts. The characters are listed in the position they held at the time of the chapter illustration.

Mr. Carson's telephone

communicates the opportunities presented by change, the technological advancements at *Downton Abbey*, and the insights and strategies in this book.

Table of Contents

Introduction

During the years surrounding WWI, societal, industrial and institutional change occurred at a rate we have not seen since. Yes, we have ongoing technological changes. For example, in the workplace, we are constantly updating our computers—yet most office employees still use a keyboard. Our cars have more instruments—but the transmission still operates much the same as the original models of the early 20th century. We keep our phones in our pockets—but we still make phone calls. We fly from continent to continent—but we still carry a paper passport. In the years surrounding WWI, the basic models of many technologies we use today were invented and introduced *en masse* to be used by businesses and people. The western world moved from a rural agricultural society to an urban industrial one. The rate of change was fundamental, monumental and revolutionary.

How did these changes happen? How were people able to cope? Compared to today, managers and employees had less formal education, little to no technical experience, and limited access to information—yet they managed to move the entire western world into the modern age. It's been suggested that they were just tougher people than we are, that they fought a world war and worked physically hard jobs—and we fail because we are soft and addicted to leisure. Perhaps they were harder working, but many of today's entrepreneurs and senior managers work in excess of 80 hours per week, so it can't be just that. There must be something more.

How is it possible with all the management theory available today, that we still have a dismal rate of success when it comes to organizational change? "More than 70% of needed change either fails to be launched, even though some people clearly see the need, fails to be completed even though someo people exhaust themselves trying, or finishes over budget, late and with initial aspirations unmet." [1] We have visioning sessions at our corporate retreats where we imagine the brave new world and then adjourn to the golf course, confident that the change will occur easily.

Perhaps we have overlooked the basics. One of the biggest differences between today's change management challenges and those at the time of *Downton Abbey* is that organizations looked and functioned very differently. Organizations had a hierarchical structure with a firm chain of command and a process to complete every task. When the work was completed, there was assessment and accountability. Managers gave direction to staff, which was followed without debate or consensus. The staff learned the new skills in a timely manner and implemented the change. Responsibility and accountability existed at every level of the organization and if an employee was unable be successful in their changed role, actions were taken.

One of the reasons change initiatives fail in organizations is because the "change agents" are often identified as a group comprised of experts, leaders, and consultants. Change management needs to happen on both a leadership and personal level. Change initiatives will only be successful if every person involved manages the change within the organization and within themselves.

The examples selected from *Downton Abbey* explore three key components to successfully managing change both personally and as a leader: Awareness, Responsibility and Choice.

Elements of this ARC model (Awareness, Responsibility, Choice) can be seen in each chapter, assisting the reader to reflect on their own experiences of change, providing insight into how team members respond to change, and supplying tools to effectively manage the change process.

The three components of ARC are:

- **Awareness** — one must be aware of what is happening in their organization, industry, society, and culture to be prepared to anticipate change and navigate it well.

- **Responsibility** — one must take responsibility for their attitudes, emotions and actions—both positive and negative.

- **Choice** — one must be proactive in acquiring all the necessary information and then make a choice.

Even within the context of lay-off, department reorganization or industry collapse, an individual still has choices. Once a person is aware of the change, there is no reason not to make decisions. Although it is tempting to perceive oneself as a victim of change, individuals have more control over their responses, actions, and outcomes than they may think.

Change in an organization presents opportunities for everyone involved: opportunities to evaluate where they are in their career, what impact the changes will have on their current role, and what new opportunities will exist in the future organization. Each person can assess what they want and what they need to do to achieve it.

Although today we think we are going through exponential change, society at the time of WWI experienced change at every level. Some organizations saw it coming and adjusted and other organizations ignored it at their peril. We can look at the examples in *Downton Abbey* and learn from their characters' success and failure when dealing with the changes in technology, workplace roles, and culture.

Change Management

The coordination
of a systematic transition
from a present state
to a future state
which proactively addresses
the effects on the organization
and the individual.

Organizational Structure & Corresponding Roles

Executive Management

(Lord Grantham, Lady Grantham, Matthew Crawley, Lady Mary Crawley)

In the organization of Downton Abbey, the executive management team also happens to be a family. The television series begins with Lord Grantham being the sole owner and functioning CEO of the estate. Eventually, he shares ownership with his son-in-law, Matthew Crawley, who invests his own money to stabilize the finances of the estate. Upon Matthew's death, his wife, Lady Mary, takes on the role of co-owner. Lady Grantham is part of the executive team as head of the household and leader of multiple community projects.

Lord Grantham
Matthew Crawley/Lady Mary Crawley

Man of Business
Mr. Murray

Agent
Mr. Jarvis/Mr. Branson

Butler
Mr. Carson

Man of Business

The Man of Business reports directly to executive management (Lord Grantham) and acts as an advisor in all legal and financial matters pertaining to the organization. He functions as a CFO and works from his London office.

Agent

The Agent oversees all tenancy contracts, businesses, and property on the land and estate. Reporting directly to executive management (Lord Grantham), he functions as a COO or General Manager.

Butler

The Butler is the most senior member of household staff, directly reporting to executive management (Lord Grantham). He is in charge of hiring, training, disciplining, and firing male staff members—specifically under butlers, valets, footmen and hall boys. He is responsible for the prudent management of resources, security of the silver, and the inventory of the wine cellar.

Lady Grantham

Housekeeper	Cook	Hospital Administrator
Mrs. Hughes	Mrs. Patmore	Dr. Clarkson

Housekeeper

The Housekeeper is head of the domestic staff, reporting directly to executive management (Lady Grantham). She is in charge of hiring, training, disciplining, and firing female staff members— specifically ladies' maids and house maids. She is responsible for the maintenance and standards of household cleanliness, ordering of inventory and security of the storeroom, cleaning and inventory of all linen, and managing the household budget and accounts.

Cook

The Cook is in charge of the kitchen department and reports directly to executive management (Lady Grantham). She is in charge of hiring, training, disciplining, and firing of kitchen staff members—specifically assistant cooks, kitchen maids and scullery maids. She is responsible for maintaining the health of family, guests, and staff through nutritional menu design and preparation of delicious, visually appealing, gourmet meals.

Hospital Administrator

The Hospital Administrator reports directly to executive management (Lady Grantham). He manages the delivery of healthcare services to the village and the maintenance and functioning of the estate-funded hospital.

Past Executive Management & Stakeholders
Dowager Countess of Grantham
Outgoing Executive Management and Hospital President

Violet Crawley, the mother of Lord Grantham, was in charge of the estate and surrounding community along with her late husband the 4th Earl of Grantham. All of the management functions and staff positions that Lady Grantham currently oversees would have been managed by the Dowager during her tenure.

Lady Edith Crawley
Second Daughter of the House

Lady Edith Crawley is a stakeholder in the affairs of the estate and household. Although she has no official managerial function or staff direct reports, she has relational authority and acts and speaks in accordance with the goals of the estate. She participates in coordinating household and community projects and represents Executive Management at functions when called upon.

Senior Management
(Butler, Housekeeper, Cook, Hospital Administrator, Agent)

The members of the senior management team report directly to executive management and have one or multiple direct reports. They oversee and manage their corresponding departments and functions and supervise the front-line managers such as under butler, assistant cook, head groom, and head gardener.

Butler
Mr. Carson

Under Butlers

Valets

Footmen
Molesley

Under Butlers

The Under Butlers report to senior management. They are responsible for the training and mentoring of footmen and junior male staff as well as tasks assigned by the senior management. They fill the position of butler when the butler is not present.

Valets

Reporting to senior management and the executive member to whom they are assigned, Valets are in charge of maintaining the wardrobe and attending to all manner of personal needs. They also provide companionship and security while travelling away from the estate.

Footmen

The Footmen report to the under butler and senior management. They are responsible for all manner of table service, opening and closing doors, delivery of messages and items, providing valet service to visitors and any additional duties as required.

Housekeeper
Mrs. Hughes

Ladies' Maids

House Maids
Gwen

Ladies' Maids

Reporting to senior management and the executive member to whom they are assigned, Ladies' Maids are in charge of maintaining the wardrobe and attending to all manner of personal needs. They also provide companionship and security while travelling away from the estate.

House Maids

House Maids report to senior management. They are responsible for the tasks and duties required to maintain the cleanliness of the house with the exception of the kitchen department and staff bedrooms.

Cook
Mrs. Patmore

Assistant Cook

Kitchen Maids
Daisy

Assistant Cook
The Assistant Cook reports to the Cook and is directly involved in the preparation and cooking of the meals including main courses, vegetables and desserts.

Kitchen Maids
The Kitchen Maids report to the cook and assistant cook. They are responsible for the cleanliness of the kitchen department including the scullery and larder. They may be called upon to clean vegetables or do additional tasks as directed. (In absence of a scullery maid, a kitchen maid may also be required to start the fires in the bedrooms or in the stove/range.)

Shifting Technology

Filter the Data
Evaluate the Costs
Recognize the Emotions
Figure It Out

"I find the whole idea
a kind of thief of life.
That people should waste hours
huddled around a wooden box,
listening to someone talking
at them, burbling inanities
from somewhere else."

Lord Grantham

Chapter One

Filter the Data

(**Awareness** — *Responsibility* — *Choice*)

ord Grantham's cousin, Lady Rose, had taken up residence at Downton Abbey while her parents served a diplomatic post in India. She, a young woman of the 1920s, was enthralled with jazz music and the new dances of the era. She used the phonograph on a regular basis and eagerly read in the newspapers about the latest technological developments of the "wireless"—the first radio. As a respectful guest at Downton Abbey, Lady Rose did not wish to be seen as rude by asking her host family to purchase a wireless. However, in an effort to persuade them, she dropped hints about how the new wireless instruments, *"are getting cheaper and more reliable"* and *"how they are more efficient now and much easier to tune"*.(3) Not in favour of the idea of purchasing a wireless, Lord Grantham initially dismissed Lady Rose's attempts to persuade him. It was not until Lady Rose asked him, *"Did you see that the King is going to speak on the wireless? ... For the opening the British Empire Exposition"*(4) , that Lord Grantham began to see the wireless may add value to the estate by providing current and useful information. Still not totally convinced of its value, Lord Grantham agreed to hire a wireless to hear the King's speech. After hearing King George V speak to the empire, Lord Grantham chose to purchase the wireless as he no longer regarded the device as a mere distraction or vehicle for wasted time.

Lord Grantham was cautious when new ideas were brought to his attention. As the CEO of the estate, he was ultimately responsible for quality of life and was on guard to keep corrupting influences out of his organization and surrounding community. This included negative influences such as technology that would compromise a healthy mind and body or the economic security of the estate and the people living on it. If there was to be technology adopted by the organization, Lord Grantham wanted to have control over the kind of technology, the type and the source of the content it provided, and the speed at which it is introduced.

Today's world is inundated with data and information which can be overwhelming. Information is available everywhere and every minute. Lord Grantham could easily control the infiltration of outside information to his family and employees by deciding against hiring or purchasing a wireless. Today's world challenges that level of control so leaders must be vigilant in understanding the power of information to influence their employees and organization. Not only did Lord Grantham believe sitting and listening to the wireless was a waste of time but that the value of the information gained was minimal.

From the introduction of the wireless, western culture has been exposed to ongoing opportunities to trade our time for useless information. Regardless of the medium, the lure of new information is powerful and on the surface, it seems the information must be valuable. The truth is that not all information is useful, and individuals and organizations need to safeguard their time and productivity against "burbling inanities". Today, it is necessary to filter incoming information not just because it may be useless—but because it may also be inaccurate and even harmful.

1. *Usefulness*

The wireless at the time of Downton Abbey brought in information and entertainment without a filter. There was only one broadcast channel — a person tuned in and heard a predetermined schedule. This programming monopoly also occurred in the early days of television. As a result, there was no way to select content one personally considered meaningful or to select content with an alternative point of view.

Although today's radio and television offers hundreds of channel choices, we now see a similar struggle for information choices in social media.(5) Users on today's popular social media sites are at the mercy of the site owner who controls the content of the news feed. Individuals may pick their friends or followers, but the media company—through its monopoly and algorithms—controls what information individuals see and how it is identified.

While undergoing change in an organization or department, it is vital for a manager to keep his team focused. A large part of this task is keeping useless data out of the employees' daily work sphere. When the internet first became widely available at individual workstations, many organizations preselected the work-related websites that employees were allowed access to and blocked those that were deemed frivolous, inappropriate, or even illegal.

Today, many employers block social media sites on company computers to reduce wasted time on non-work-related activity. The effectiveness of this practice has been reduced with the advent of smart phones that can be used surreptitiously or when employees feign that social media needs to be accessed for them to do their work. In addition, managers need to be aware that maintaining corporate social media sites may be used as a claim by employees to justify low priority activity or procrastinate from assigned duties.

2. Accuracy

Online information is instant and what is shared the most filters to the top of the news feed. It is a common mistake to assume a story that "goes viral" is accurate—when it may be completely inaccurate and its popularity only a result of the human desire for the salacious. An information item employees source through social media about their organization or industry may be a popular search result but still may be inaccurate. The danger is that employees may be using this data to inform their choices.

3. Safety

One of the greater risks presented by social media in the workplace is the lure and seducing nature intrinsic in its design. Some employees simply find it very difficult to disengage once connected.

High use of social media such as Facebook, Twitter and Instagram correlates to a decrease in real life social community participation and an increase in relationship problems.[6] The appeal of social media may be traced to its reflection of today's individualist culture. On these social media sites, the individual is the focus of attention and it is this egocentrism that has been linked to internet addiction. Social media allows individuals to present themselves positively to the outside world which enhances their mood state and this pleasurable feeling facilitates the drive to addiction.[7] The rapid pace of change in this type of technology requires all leaders to be aware of the effect of this change and put in place appropriate social media policies. Individuals who take responsibility for the outcome of their social media use and make appropriate decisions will be less inclined to be negatively affected as technology continues to make people alive online and invisible in real life.

If you are a manager, consider these tips for filtering the data:

1. Regularly post organizational news in employee staff rooms or online employee forums so that employees are as informed as possible.

2. Encourage questions regarding changes in the organization and industry. Make this information part of management meetings so front-line supervisors have the answers at their fingertips.

3. Determine when, if at all, social media devices are allowed within the hours of work. Communicate this restriction in position postings, hiring interviews, and new hire orientation.

4. Have a social media policy that details:

   • what employees can post or share about the organization and its customers, coworkers, leaders, and their own role within the organization

   • times and locations when social media devices may be used during work hours.

Social media use in the workplace may cost organizations productivity due to employee overuse, brand damage due to inaccurate information, or employee cohesion as employees increasingly desire to be a team member only online.

*"The telephone is not a toy,
but a useful
and valuable tool."*

Mr. Carson

Chapter Two

Evaluate the Costs

(Awareness — Responsibility — **Choice***)*

ord Grantham ordered two telephones installed at Downton Abbey. With the looming anticipation of war, he wanted to ensure the estate had the benefit of the new technology prior to rationing. One was installed in the upstairs hall and one in the butler's pantry. Initially, Mr. Carson was reluctant to accept the introduction of the telephone but was convinced by Lord Grantham's argument, *"The telephone is here now ... besides none of us know what the next few months will bring."* [9] The staff members were excited and intrigued by this new technology and asked Mr. Carson how it worked. Mr. Carson quickly reminded them that the telephone was brought into the house as a tool and not an amusement.

By the final season of *Downton Abbey*, more than a decade has passed since Lord Grantham first installed the telephone. Lord Grantham's sister, Lady Rosamund was a trustee of the new women's college, Hillcroft. She had recommended Lady Edith as a trustee and they invited the treasurer, Mr. Harding, to Downton Abbey to discuss the college and its mandate. Mr. Harding lived in a different county than Hillcroft. When asked by Lady Edith how he managed to work as treasurer of Hillcroft from an office in a different county, he responded, *"It's not that hard, I go there twice a month. But the telephone has really changed everything."* [10] In the decade following the installment of the telephone at Downton Abbey, this new communication tool became commonplace in both business and private houses. It revolutionized business and personal relationships by allowing individuals to communicate ear-to-ear over distance.

Whether the change is to install telephones a century ago or purchasing new software applications today, organizations and individuals need to assess the true value of each new technology:

1. Is this change in alignment with our brand? Will it build the brand or diminish it?

2. Will this new technology further assist us in reaching our goals and fulfill the mission of our core business?

3. Is this a short-term solution to a long term problem? Based on our current processes, is this something that should be addressed now or in the future?

4. What will be the positive benefits and negative impacts of this technology on our customers, employees, investors, and environment? Who are the winners and losers in this change?

5. How is this new technology an improvement over our existing technology?

6. Is the net gain of the improvement worth the learning curve and chaos of implementing this change?

7. Are the right people making this decision or are there internal and external voices at the table that do not belong there? Is the vendor's offer driving this proposed change?

8. Overall, will this technology provide benefits in increased sales and efficiency equal or greater than the outlay of cost for purchase, training, and implementation?

Evaluating all potential technology changes through a lens of money, time, and results—both gained and lost—will help an organization maintain the course of their mandate and maximize productivity.

"But Daisy mustn't find out
that I don't know how to work it
... because it makes her
part of the future
and leaves me stuck in the past."

Mrs. Patmore

Chapter Three
Recognize the Emotions

(Awareness — Responsibility — Choice)

ady Grantham asked Lady Edith, when she was next in London, to purchase an electric mixer for the kitchen staff at Downton Abbey. Daisy, the Assistant Cook, was excited to examine the new labour saving machine and decided to use it to make the mousse for the evening's dinner. However, Mrs. Patmore looked at the machine with trepidation, said, *"Oh, my God. We'd better have some soup put by. I'd rather not rely on that contraption."* (12) Daisy's machine-made mousse was praised as delicious at dinner.

Later that evening, with no witnesses to her learning attempt, Mrs. Patmore tried to use the new machine. She inserted the prongs incorrectly, which caused the bowl to dislodge and crash to the floor and break. Mrs. Hughes heard the crash and came into the kitchen to investigate. Mrs. Hughes suggested Mrs. Patmore leave the mess for Daisy to clean up the next morning, but Mrs. Patmore confessed she needed to learn how to use the mixer. She wanted to be part of the future, even though it frightened her. Mrs. Hughes empathized and helped Mrs. Patmore clean up the mess.

Although Daisy and Mrs. Patmore were both exposed to the new machine in their work environment at the same time, their initial response was dramatically different, perhaps as a result of their age.

Renowned British author and humourist, Douglas Adams, in his last book, *Salmon of Doubt*, explores this concept of acceptance of change and age.[13] *"I've come up with a set of rules that describe our reactions to technologies:*

1. *Anything that is in the world when you're born is normal and ordinary and is just a natural part of the way the world works.*

2. *Anything that's invented between when you're fifteen and thirty-five is new and exciting and revolutionary and you can probably get a career in it.*

3. *Anything invented after you're thirty-five is against the natural order of things."*

As in Adams' description above, Daisy's response was characteristic of a young person. The mixer was exciting and revolutionary, and she could see how it would positively impact her role and decrease her labour. The older Mrs. Patmore was skeptical of this new machine and she found it, in Adams' term, *"against the natural order"*. Mrs. Patmore soon realized, however, that ignoring this new tool might mean her methods of managing the kitchen would eventually become obsolete, so she embarked on a late-night learning expedition.

Although in this example, Mr. Adams' generalized theory rings true, many young people today resist change while some older employees are fascinated and eager to embrace new ideas and technology, particularly in their area of interest or expertise.

People respond to change differently and the best way for leaders to manage change is to become aware of these different emotional responses to change so they can coach employees effectively.[14]

Enthusiast — a person who is truly enthusiastic about the change. They believe it will be an improvement for themselves, others and the organization. *"This is going to be great!"*

Cheerleader — a person who supports the change because the decision has been made by the appropriate authority and it is their job to look for the benefits and work towards its success. *"We can do this. What's first?"*

Self-Promoter — a person who recognizes the change is inevitable and actively supports the process in order to control any positive and negative impacts to self. *"I volunteer to handle the department relocation. Should I draw up a list of who gets which office space?"*

Passive Aggressor — a person who will outwardly support the change but works to undermine its implementation. *"Sounds like a good idea, but I have heard a lot of staff are upset and won't support this."*

Dazed and Confused — a person who resists the change with confusion. They ask for multiple explanations and rational for the change and resist seeing the justification behind the decision. *"I don't understand. Explain it to me again. How will this merger create that outcome?"*

Stalled Learner — a person who resists the change by not learning necessary tools and processes to implement the change. *"I just can't get SAP to print the reports I need. Can't I still just use Peoplesoft?"*

Drama Student — a person who resists the change by acting overly emotional when asked to implement the change. *"I just can't deal with this. I think I have to go home. I have a migraine. This is very stressful!"*

Obstructionist — a person who deliberately refuses to support or implement the change because they assume they know better than the legitimate authority in charge. *"This reorganization is the wrong move. Someone has to say it — so I will!"*

In the model of emotional response above, Daisy could be considered an *Enthusiast* and Mrs. Patmore *a Stalled Learner*. Throughout the *Downton Abbey* series, Mrs. Patmore is reluctant to adopt new technology. The television show does not reveal to what extent she masters this kitchen appliance. As the manager of her department, she could just delegate this task to her assistant cook, Daisy.

Individuals who respond negatively to change may not be conscious of the effect of their attitudes and behaviour. Resisting change unconsciously will undermine success for an individual, but once the individual becomes aware of their emotional response to change, they can take responsibility for their emotional state, their choices and their future.

"You have to
set the number on the dial
and I had it up too high,
but I've got the hang of it now."

Mrs. Hughes

Chapter Four

Figure It Out

(Awareness — **Responsibility** *— Choice)*

rs. Hughes purchased an electric toaster and was eager to see how it worked. Mr. Carson came upon her as she removed it from the box and asked what it was. Mrs. Hughes replied, *"An electric toaster. I've given it to myself as a treat. If it's any good, I'm going to suggest getting one for the upstairs breakfasts."*[16] Mr. Carson was not enthused.

While experimenting with the device later in the day, Mrs. Hughes inadvertently burned some toast, which filled her sitting room smoke. Seeing the smoke drifting into the hallway, Mr. Carson grabbed a bucket of sand and rushed into Mrs. Hughes' room to extinguish the expected fire. Fanning the smoke above the toaster, Mrs. Hughes quickly explained there was no fire or need for sand. She discovered through trial and error that if the dial is set too high, the toast would burn.

As noted in the previous chapter, Mrs. Hughes could be described as an *Enthusiast*. A leader who was truly enthusiastic about the change, she believed the toaster would be an improvement for herself, fellow staff and the organization. Mr. Carson, when managing the introduction of the telephone in a previous episode, could have been described as a *Cheerleader*. A leader who supported the change because the decision had been made by the appropriate authority, he recognized it was his job to seek the benefits and work towards success.

Mr. Carson moved quickly into the role of *Cheerleader* even though he was not eager to learn to use the telephone.

As a senior manager, he knew it was his responsibility to figure how to use the new tool even if it meant looking foolish:

Mr. Carson takes the telephone earpiece reverently and speaks.

Mr. Carson: "Hello. This is Downton Abbey. Carson, the butler, speaking."

He reviews his performance and tries again.

Mr. Carson: "Hello. This is Mr. Carson, the butler of Downton Abbey. To whom am I speaking?"

To his amazement there is someone at the other end.

Mr. Carson: "What? I am not shouting! Who are you? Oh. Mrs. Gaunt. No, I don't want to place a call ... I was practicing my answer ... well, I dare say a lot of the things you do sound stupid to other people!" [17]

Unlike the situation with Mrs. Hughes who was enthusiastic about introducing a new change on her own, Mr. Carson was not enthusiastic—but he felt responsible to take initiative, to learn, and to implement the change.

When a responsible person says he will perform a job, he will try to accomplish what is asked — both for the organization and so that he may gain a measure of self-worth. An irresponsible person may or may not do what he says he will do—his actions depend on how he feels, the effort he has to make, and what is in it for him. He neither gains self-respect, nor the respect of the others. In time, he will suffer or cause others to suffer due to his irresponsibility. [18]

Whether leaders are implementing technological change like Mrs. Hughes or adapting to a change like Mr. Carson, they are responsible to investigate the technology and acquire the knowledge and skill to operate it in a timely manner.

Change in organizations requires initiative as a key competency for a leader. As former CEO of General Electric Jack Welch said, "When *the rate of change inside an institution becomes slower than the rate of change outside, the end is in sight. The only question is when."*[19]

Successfully managing change requires selecting people based on their level of initiative and follow-through. But how does a leader identify which employee can take responsibility to proactively learn and figure it out? Most people would evaluate themselves as having initiative but driving change in a fast paced work environment requires people who are at the top of this bell curve.

Here are some questions to use when selecting team members:

1. Have they sought out new opportunities or responsibilities, even risky ones?

2. Do they seek out learning that has not been pre-arranged by their leader or company?

3. Do they easily transfer knowledge from one experience into wisdom that could be used in alternate situations?

4. Have they pushed through difficult or complicated tasks to completion?

To manage technological change effectively, leaders must take initiative, model initiative, expect initiative, and reward initiative.

Shifting Roles

Change the People
Find the People
Move On
Make the Change
Create Your Opportunity

"*Sir Anthony,*
it must be so hard to meet
the challenge of the future,
and yet be fair
to your employees."

Lady Edith Crawley

Chapter Five

Change the People

*(Awareness — Responsibility — **Choice**)*

ord and Lady Grantham hosted a dinner party for a couple of neighbours. Before long, the conversation turned to agriculture—their common industry. Sir Anthony Strallan had purchased a harvester and said, *"The next few years in farming are going to be about mechanization. That's the test and we're going to have to meet it."*(21) He was aware this new machinery required a level of skill which several of his current farm workers did not possess.

Lady Edith, intrigued by what Sir Anthony was saying, responded from across the dining table, *"It must be so hard to meet the challenge of the future, and yet be fair to your employees."*(22) Understanding the emotional reality that comes with adopting change, he agreed with Lady Edith, *"This is the point, precisely. We can't fight progress, but we must find ways to soften the blow."*(23)

Often change brings about a need for different skills in the workplace. However, many leaders neglect the transitional planning, training, and recruitment needed to ensure the organization has the skilled workforce required.

This workforce can be made up of existing employees that currently have these skills, those who learn the skills on their own, those who are taught the skills by company training, and those who are hired from outside and bring these skills with them. It is important to consider each of these groups as sources for the changed organization as it is unlikely a leader can secure the productive staff they need only from within their current employee group.

In the *Downton Abbey* example, Sir Anthony recognizes he has to match his employee base to the new mechanized organization and that is where the real challenge lies. He knows this means that some of his current employees will be displaced by this change and that the change process must be managed fairly and compassionately.

Here are three steps for a manager to assess skill level:

Measure the Gap — Define the skills and knowledge needed for success in the future state. Evaluate the current workforce skill and knowledge level. Identify the expertise and skills which are missing.

Measure the Talent — Evaluate individual employee's skills and aptitude based on the requirement of the future state—not based on what individuals have done in the past or do currently. Assess their willingness to learn the new skills required. Confirm their capacity to learn these skills.

Measure the Commitment — When designing the transitional learning and implementation plan, include in each phase a responsibility and accountability benchmark that will ensure renewed commitment to the project and increased confidence for the employee.

Good organizations acknowledge and provide effective and compassionate outplacement services to those employees who cannot or choose not to be part of the future state.

*"So I told them
I will do it,
I will drive the tractor."*

Lady Edith Crawley

Chapter Six

Find the People

(Awareness — Responsibility — Choice)

s WWI waged on, many young men were called up to fight, leaving a labour shortage across the country. One night at dinner, Lady Edith informed Lord and Lady Grantham and the Dowager Countess that she had spoken to Mrs. Drake. The Drakes were the estate's tenant farmers at Longfield Farm. Lady Edith said, *"Apparently, their final able-bodied farmhand has been called up. They need a man to drive the tractor."*[25] She further explained that Mr. Drake did not drive and so she volunteered to drive the tractor for them.

Lady Edith had taken the initiative to learn to drive before the war began, leaving her as one of the few people left on the estate who could drive. She was confident in her skill and had a genuine desire to help. Lord Grantham was pleased that Lady Edith was willing to fill this role and use her driving skills for the good of the organization.

The Drakes needed a farm hand that could drive the tractor and Lady Edith was an unlikely candidate for this role. The Drakes would have been looking for a traditional candidate—a young man with a farming background. This demographic exemplified the labour pool from which farm worker candidates were typically drawn. It is only because of the war occurring at this time that candidates from this demographic were not plentiful.

Women have always worked in the paid labour force but have not always worked in the breadth of roles that their male counterparts have. Prior to WWI, women did not work in transportation roles. Men were the chauffeurs, the mechanics, the bus drivers, and the train engineers. In today's world, women are moving into more non-traditional roles every day, even though some managers still do not initially consider women as qualified candidates for non-traditional or blue-collar jobs. In Lady Edith's case, it was a win-win. She enhanced her driving skills by operating both an automobile and now a tractor—the organization gained a competent worker in a skilled role.

In today's business environment, labour shortages in specific industries and job categories require organizations to source candidates from alternative demographics. When the gap is measured to build the organizational team to navigate change, leaders need to consider employee groups not usually evaluated.

Contrary to common belief, not all baby boomers are rushing to retirement. Many continue in the workforce for various reasons: they find work meaningful and want to continue contributing, they still require income due to reduced pension and retirement benefits, or they jump back in as a consultant due to an organizational request for their expertise. An older employee from another company may be just who you need for a six-month implementation. The staff member you want for your five-year plan may be a candidate who is 60 years old versus a Gen Y.

One of the benefits of modern technology today is that organizations can source employees that would otherwise be geographically unavailable. With the world getting smaller and air travel becoming more affordable, hiring engineers from India and China has now become a more frequent occurrence. Employees can be sourced from across the globe or across the country.

For many years, the Alberta energy industry has relied on workers from the Canadian maritime provinces. This has been beneficial to both parties—the energy sector gains skilled labour and the employees receive highly skilled, year-round jobs.

Whether you are changing the people or finding the people—when undergoing organizational change—you need to recruit beyond your usual demographic and traditional labour pools. Your employees of the future may not look like your employees of the past.

"Service is ending for most of us
... there's going to be
more and more people
chasing fewer and fewer jobs."

Molesley

Chapter Seven

Move On

(Awareness — Responsibility — Choice)

hen Molesley was a child, he was a bright student and his father thought he had the makings of a teacher. However, when Molesley's mother died, he was forced to leave school early and work to help support the family, eventually ending up in a career of domestic service. His genuine interest in education and knowledge followed him into adulthood and he continued to pursue education through self-directed learning.

Molesley mentored Daisy, the assistant cook, after her tutor left the village. While working with Mr. Dawes, the Downton Village schoolmaster, to arrange Daisy's examinations, Molesley inadvertently impressed the schoolmaster with his high regard for education. Mr. Dawes, wanting to harness this enthusiasm, asked Molesley to sit a general knowledge exam to ascertain whether Molesley would be qualified to join his teaching staff.

After correcting Molesley's exam, Mr. Dawes reported that Molesley's knowledge exceeded some Cambridge and Oxford graduates and he was pleased to offer him a teaching position at the village school. This was serendipitous because although Molesley had risen to the top in his field of domestic service as a butler, he was already forced to take a position as footman because service positions were slowly being eliminated.

Daisy, excited for Mr. Molesley's new opportunity:

Daisy: *"Is that the end of service for you?"*

Molesley: *"Service is ending for most of us, Daisy. I've just got a head start."*

Daisy: *"Will you miss it?"*

Molesley: *"Well let's face it—I (was) never going to make Butler. Well, not in a proper house like this one. And from now on, there's going to be more and more people chasing fewer and fewer jobs. So it's probably time, and this seems like a good way to go."* (27)

Like the service employees at the time of *Downton Abbey,* many types of jobs have come and gone. Consider the elevator operator who kindly asked which floor, closed the door and pushed the button. Or the washroom attendant that directed customers to an empty stall and handed them a towel at the sink. The telephone operator who inquired which name to be contacted and connected the call with polite dispatch. The whip and harness makers whose handcrafted items were ubiquitous on every carriage and buggy. Consider the milkman, who in the early hours before dawn, delivered specific orders of cold milk to small doors at the side of homes, collected the coins left in payment and the list for the next day's purchase.

On the horizon there may be a reduction in delivery drivers with the advent of drone delivery technology. With the onset of online retain purchasing, we may see the closure of physical retail outlets because their high physical overhead costs make them uncompetitive.

Products and services have come and gone. What is fashionable today may not be tomorrow. As technology increases and society changes, entire job categories simply disappear or exist in highly reduced numbers.

The example of Molesley shows us that when change brings about a loss of vocation or role, we need to look at all of our experience and skills to evaluate alternate career paths. Take inventory of what you can do and what you know and see where the hidden opportunities may lay. Molesley was surprised how his past experience and knowledge could deliver him into a career that he thought was only a dream.

*"I've bought a typewriter
and I've taken a postal course
in shorthand ...
Because I want to leave service.
I want to be a secretary."*

Gwen

Chapter Eight

Make the Change

(Awareness — Responsibility — Choice)

y the mid-19th century, the increasing pace of business communication had created a need for mechanization of the writing process. The first commercial typewriters were introduced in 1874 and became common in offices over the next several decades. Gwen, a housemaid at Downton Abbey, recognized this new field of work and sought to acquire the typing and shorthand skills necessary to become a professional secretary.

After putting money away for some time, she spent most of her savings on the purchase of a typewriter and enrolled in a correspondence class in shorthand. Gwen practiced and completed her course work on her own time and kept her aspirations private. When her coworker confiscated her typewriter without Gwen's knowledge and revealed the machine to Gwen's boss and the other staff, she found herself having to explain and defend her career plan.

Managing change sometimes means you have to take initiative and ask yourself, *"How can I be a part of this exciting future?"* Asking this question is the first step but it alone will not ensure you reach your goal. A person has to behave in a way that will propel them forward towards their goal and not allow them to fall back into fear and doubt.

William Glasser offers a useful metaphor for staying on the road to our goal. He explains, "The four easily recognizable components that together make up total behaviour are as follows:

Doing — walking, talking or moving

Thinking — what we think and what we say to ourselves

Feeling — positive emotions such as joy or negative emotions such as anger

Physiology — unconscious behaviour such as sweating, posture and general health of your body." (29)

According to Glasser, each of these four components are like the tires of an automobile—if they are not all properly and evenly inflated, you will fail to move forward or, worse yet, spin in circles. If you want to keep moving forward to your goal, be sure that you are aware and responsibly choosing how you think, how you feel, what you do, and how you manage your physiology.

At one moment, when confronted by her colleagues, Gwen allowed her thinking and feeling "tires" to deflate. She could have *thought, acted* and *felt* herself out of her goal. With flat tires, she would have found herself in the ditch and no longer on the road to her goal.

Doing — Once Gwen decided she wanted to be a secretary, she took these specific actions:

- Saved up and bought a typewriter which was an expensive investment in her future
- Enrolled in a course while working full time
- Learned the skills at a level of competency that would allow her to compete for a job
- Defended goals when challenged and derided by her current colleagues
- Sold her skillset effectively.

Thinking — We can presume that Gwen would have spent a great deal of time thinking about this plan—just in researching and purchasing the typewriter alone.

Feeling — At times Gwen was discouraged by not finding a position she wanted, *"I suppose I've just realized that it's not going to happen ... I'm not going to be a secretary ... I'm lucky to be a maid."*[30] However, part of her success in keeping her tires inflated was having an encouraging team of friends and coworkers that supported and encouraged her to stay on the road to her goal.

Physiology — Gwen managed her health, maintaining the physical strength and mental capacity to do her full-time job as well as complete her training and practice her new skills.

The power in learning what drives an individual's behavior is that it allows that person to then direct their behavior. With this knowledge, individuals are more effective in satisfying their needs and reaching their goals. Like Gwen who saw the opportunity and achieved her goal in becoming a secretary, an individual's key to making change is to look for opportunity, learn what needs to be learned, and do what needs to be done.

*"Well, I'll rent it out now
and, then later,
I thought I might take in
some lodgers."*

Mrs. Patmore

Chapter Nine
Create Your Opportunity

(Awareness — Responsibility — Choice)

rs. Patmore's aunt had passed away and left her an inheritance of a few hundred quid, which was more money than she had ever been able to save. She wanted to invest the money in a reliable way to build for her future. She sought advice from Mr. Carson, who suggests she invest in a building company in Thirsk.

Mrs. Patmore was reluctant to put her money into an investment she knew nothing about, and she chose to purchase a property which would provide rental income today and a place to live in her retirement. As Mrs. Patmore considered her property and its potential, she realized with her expertise and her niece's labour, she could open a bed and breakfast hotel. This business would make more profit than monthly rental alone. Mrs. Patmore's plans evolved from growing her money to generating revenue to creating a business.

When Mrs. Patmore set about deciding on what to do with her investment, she gathered facts, listened to her instincts, identified the faults, focused on the benefits, thought of what the purchase could lead to, and stepped back and evaluated the big picture. Although she wasn't consciously aware of her process, it was very similar to a decision making process for change management used worldwide called the **Six Thinking Hats** by Edward de Bono.[32]

De Bono identified six areas where our brain may focus when making decisions about a change: managing, information, emotions, discernment, optimistic response, and creativity.

Most people have a default area of focus when thinking only at an unconscious level. Decisions are made quickly, based on the most familiar way of thinking. However, no one area of thought can provide the necessary information to make a good decision in a fast-changing environment.

The **Six Thinking Hats** process gives the thinker the opportunity to consider all six areas of focus before making a choice—with the goal of making the best decision. There are six metaphorical colored hats, each one associated with a different area of focus regarding the idea. The thinker "puts on" each hat to ensure they have considered the information from all six areas:

White Hat of Information: look for the data. What do we know about this issue? What don't we know?

Red Hat of Emotion: look at the issue using intuition, gut reaction, and emotion. How do you feel about this decision and how do others feel who may be affected by it?

Yellow Hat of Optimism: look at the decision positively. What are the benefits of this idea? What is great about it?

Green Hat of Creativity: look at this decision creatively. What could this idea lead to?

Blue Hat of Management: look at the big picture. What is the goal? How does this tie to our mission or mandate?

Black Hat of Discernment: look at a decision's flaws and risks, cautiously and defensively. How might this not work out? What could go wrong? Is it realistic and practical?

When Mrs. Patmore asked Mr. Carson about the possible investment in Thirsk, *"Can you buy shares in W.P.Moss? I mean, have they gone public?"* [33], she was looking for facts and data to aid her in making her decision. **(White Hat)**

When Mrs. Patmore tells Mr. Carson that she has decided to buy a house to rent out, Mr. Carson chides her for making such a safe and small choice compared to investing in the building industry. However, Mrs. Patmore feels the purchase is a big step and replies, "*It's £300, so it's a big decision, but you have given me the courage.*"(34) **(Red Hat)**

Mrs. Patmore saw the possibility of purchasing the house. "*Well I'll rent it now and, then later, I thought I might take in some lodgers. It's got three bedrooms.*"(35) **(Yellow Hat)**

She went beyond just the positive outcome of the purchase and taking in borders to what she could create—a bed and breakfast hotel. "*I turned one bedroom into a bathroom and installed an inside privy. It leaves me two bedrooms to let and one for my niece to run it.*"(36) **(Green Hat)**

Mrs. Patmore realized she needed to manage the marketing of the business and told Mrs. Hughes, "*I have put an advertisement in the papers. I've installed a telephone in the house.*"(37) **(Blue Hat)**

De Bono's **Six Thinking Hats** is a powerful technique for making a choice involving change. Although Mrs. Patmore was not aware of this technique, she unconsciously incorporated much of the model in her decision to buy her bed and breakfast hotel.

Shifting Culture

Keep the House in Order
Mind the Surroundings
Sell the Change
Do No Harm
Make It Stick

"*The estate
has been run
very wastefully.*"

Matthew Crawley

Chapter Ten

Keep the House in Order

(Awareness — Responsibility — Choice)

n the following *Downton Abbey* example, both Lord Grantham and the Estate Agent, Jarvis, had been negligent in keeping the organization moving forward in a productive, profitable manner. Lord Grantham was perfectly happy to allow Jarvis to continue to run the estate with minimum input and effort on his own part. When Mr. Murray, his Man of Business, continuously brought up changes that needed to be made or challenges that needed to be met, Lord Grantham shrugged off his advisor's concerns.

The details regarding the mismanagement of the estate became clear to Matthew Crawley after he invested his inheritance from Mr. Squire (his late fiancé's father). As a new member of the Executive Management team, Matthew attempted to raise the issue with Lord Grantham, who consistently minimized Matthew's concerns and ignored his request to discuss the operations of the organization.

Eventually Lord Grantham agreed to attend a meeting with Jarvis, Mr. Murray, and Matthew:(39)

Mathew: *"Thanks to Mr. Squire, we have another chance, but we have to change our ways. All I'm talking about is investment, increasing productivity, and reducing waste."*

Jarvis: *"Waste!"*

Matthew: *"Yes. The estate has been run very wastefully for many years."*

Jarvis: *"I won't listen to this!"*

Lord Grantham: *"Now, come on, Jarvis. If I can listen to it, so can you."*

Jarvis: "*No, Lord Grantham, I can't! Am I to stand here, after forty years of loyal service, to be accused of malfeasance and corruption!*"

Matthew: "*Nothing of the sort!*"

Jarvis: "*I'm the old broom, Mr. Crawley. You are the new. I wish you luck with your sweeping.*"

An organization in which all levels are engaged productively, profitably, and effectively to achieve its clear mission and goals is one with its "house in order". This philosophy allows an organization to be poised to take advantage of changing circumstances. A challenge in keeping your organization "in order" is the abdication of authority, the rubberstamping of management action, and the discounting of valid information about the state of the organization.

According to Jeffrey A. Sonnenfeld, writing in Harvard Business Review, "*It is the responsibility of the board to insist that it receive adequate information.*"[40] It is difficult for an organization to quickly and effectively change if those in senior leadership—whether at the board, executive, or senior management level—are uninformed as to the true state of their organization or choose not to act upon that information.

In the *Downton Abbey* example, Lord Grantham lived his life in blissful ignorance of the true condition of the estate, acting when disaster loomed, but otherwise expecting his CEO (Estate Agent Jarvis) to lead without his direction or input. His Man of Business (Mr. Murray) consistently brought to his attention areas of concern, which Lord Grantham discounted or disregarded. His reluctance to discuss the financial reality of the estate with his new investor, Matthew Crawley, further illustrated his desire to distance himself from necessary oversight and day-to-day guidance of the organization.

A further leadership failure was Lord Grantham's willingness to "rubber stamp" Jarvis' decisions. This choice to acquiesce to senior management and abdicate authority is not an uncommon behaviour for a board director. According to Judith Miller, writing in Non-profit Management & Leadership, *"Even when evidence suggests that boards should be more diligent in their oversight responsibilities, deference to the chief executive seems to be the default."* (41)

Like in the situation above, proactive oversight is made more difficult when employees react personally and negatively. Jarvis, who had not received negative feedback or course correction for decades, was shocked and reacted emotionally rather than providing the requested information in a professional manner. When oversight has been ignored year after year and accountability is finally brought to bear, employees may feel betrayed at this change of management style.

When change inevitably arrives, the challenges it brings will be magnified if organizations lose, through poor leadership, key players and their intellectual capital, corporate memory, and skill sets.

This example from *Downton Abbey* is a conversation that happens at the Executive Management level, but leaders at every level are responsible for effective administration of their departments.

Questions to evaluate if the "house is in order" or if leadership is "asleep at the wheel" in the organization:

1. Does the organization have a culture that is complacent or one that is prepared for change?
2. Are leadership and staff in a position to respond positively to change? Is the reaction more likely to be personal and negative?
3. Can the organization act in a timely manner to respond to and embrace change?
4. Has the organization done the work of keeping processes, documentation, training, and technology up to date?
5. Is the messaging in the company change friendly?
6. Are leaders positive influences and advocates for change?
7. What actions must be completed before we even begin?

Processes, documentation, training and technology must be kept up to date because when change comes—whether as a crisis or an opportunity—there will not be time to organize the house first.

"The wage bill is three times what it was before the war. Soon, it will be worse."

Lord Grantham

Chapter Eleven
Mind the Surroundings

(Awareness — Responsibility — Choice)

n the years surrounding WWI, society experienced exponential and widespread change. While there were many changes occurring at a political and societal level, organizations were also drastically affected by labour costs, taxation issues, and the introduction of labour saving machines.

Lord Grantham and his mother, the Dowager, discussed how these changes were affecting the estate:

Lord Grantham: *"To be honest, I am starting to ask myself, how much longer we can go on with it all. The household, the servants."*

Dowager: *"You're not in difficulties, are you?"*

Lord Grantham: *"No. But a butler, under butler, footmen, a valet, ladies' maids? To say nothing of the housemaids, the kitchen, the laundry, the gardens ..."*

Dowager: *"You think it is a bit too much in 1925?"*

Lord Grantham: *"The wage bill is three times what it was before the war. Soon, it will be worse. And anyway, who lives as we used to now? ... Most people are cutting down."* (43)

Lord Grantham was considering a reduction of staff not due to a financial crisis, but in an effort to mitigate the ever-increasing cost of labour that could no longer be justified based on the current and future needs of the estate. He was mindful of the critical factors affecting his industry and he was eager to keep the estate moving forward and stay current with the economic trends regarding input and wage costs.

The business model of Downton Abbey was completely re-engineered in the decade following WWI. Some of these changes were very painful for Lord Grantham, but he now proactively looked to his surroundings to see what was on the horizon politically, economically, demographically, and culturally that could impact his business. Lord Grantham had transformed from a negligent leader to a diligent, informed, and proactive one in less than a decade.

A leader minding his surroundings at the time of *Downton Abbey* would have seen four major trends:

1.   Political/Regulatory

The change in the British government prior to WWI brought about a political will and legislative desire to increase the death tax on the aristocracy in an effort to redistribute income. The effect of this tax change was one of the main financial factors in the re-engineering of Lord Grantham's estate from a business model of tenancy to one of intensive farming.

Death taxes—or estate duties—originally introduced in Britain to pay off the deficit and to fund the Napoleonic wars, were introduced in 1859 at 7%.[44] In 1909, in addition to the current death tax rate, the British government of the day imposed a 20% tax on the unearned increase in value of land (capital gains) and a 50% tax on undeveloped land and minerals—both payable at death of the owner or sale of the land.[45] The death tax rate continued to rise sharply following WWI to 40% by 1925. It doubled in the two decades following, landing at 80% by 1949, crippling historical agricultural state businesses.[46]

At the time of *Downton Abbey*, land owners were aware of the existing death tax, but the rapid increase of its rate and the introduction of additional land-related taxes left many businesses with insufficient time to manage the changes necessary to survive.[47]

On July 1st, 2014, Canadian Anti-Spam Legislation (CASL) was introduced. Businesses in general were pleased to see some of the elements of this legislation such as an end to installing computer programs without the express consent of the owner or collecting personal information by accessing an electronic device illegally. However, they were shocked by the economic impact of CASL's demand to cease sending commercial electronic messages (email) without express consent of the owners. Overnight, entire marketing strategies became illegal and organizations found themselves forbidden to use this effective and profitable strategy.

2. *Economic*

Due to the growing economy following WWI and its corresponding increase in different kinds of work in developing and expanding industries, people had more choices as to the kind of work they could do and the organizations they could work for. These new opportunities in factories and retail environments created a competitive increase in wages and benefits offered.

Following the war, the senior management at Downton Abbey (Mr. Carson and Mrs. Hughes) began to see staff leaving their organization for positions in shops, offices, and factories in urban environments. The reasons given were primarily due to the benefit of a structured work week with more leisure time offered by these new positions; jobs in service and agriculture required staff to live where they worked and be available day and night.

Lord Grantham was aware of the increase in wages demanded to keep quality staff. In light of this competitive job market, he was considering reducing his staff numbers, in order to pay the remaining staff competitive wages.

In today's business environment, employees continue to value the benefit of choosing when and where they work. Imagine if employers twenty years ago foresaw the trend towards flextime and work-from-home arrangements—what different decisions would they have made regarding acquiring office space and even parking spots? Would they build a new office as their business grows even though their onsite staff has stayed the same or decreased?

3. *Demographic*

The loss of life of able-bodied workmen due to the First World War dramatically shifted the demographic base of working age employees across Britain. Many businesses suffered trying to find available and qualified employees. The previous business model of the estate, based on tenant farming, required a high number of farm labourers. Had Lord Grantham continued with this labour-intensive business model, he may have struggled with a labour shortage as well. However, as a result of re-engineering his business model to intensive farming, his new business plan and operations included many labour saving machines which saved him from that fate.

In the decade following the introduction of the gas-fueled tractor in 1910, this machine became widely used in areas of intensive farming. [48] The tractor made a major impact on the social and economic fabric by increasing the productivity of agricultural labor. Mechanization freed up farm operators, unpaid family workers, and farm hands.

Many of these people relocated to the growing cities across the country and provided technically skilled, hard-working labour to the manufacturing and service industries. The landscape of the country had changed as a result. Farms grew larger, as one proprietor could manage to cultivate the land that several families would have worked in 1900. [49]

The desire to attract available and qualified employees is a continuing concern in today's organizations. In North America, the human resource shortage in the healthcare, services, and technology sectors has been circumvented by immigration. However, many immigrants today speak English as a second or third language. Due to this language barrier, although the employees may be available, they are not as qualified to function in the positions as the roles have historically been performed.

Consider the fast food giant, McDonalds, and their latest move to distance their customers from their employees through the use of technology in order to circumvent the language barrier inherent in using immigrant labour. Although in a recent Forbes magazine article, McDonalds claims its "experience of the future" which includes self-serve kiosks and ordering via mobile phone is driven by a desire to increase customer service, it also solves the core problem presented by a non-English speaking workforce. McDonalds's new technology increases its profit by moving more customers through an automated versus personalized process, thereby eliminating the need to invest in language training for their employees. [50]

4. *Cultural/Societal*

At the time of *Downton Abbey*, a major cultural change in how people purchased personal goods occurred. This social change was driven from both the top and the bottom of society.

With the development of pre-sewn garments sold from the rack, members of the wealthy class had an alternative to their dressmakers and tailors. At the same time, poor and lower income citizens who were moving into the middle class and experiencing the power of income growth in the post-war environment could now afford to purchase pre-sewn garments instead of relying on making the items themselves.

Like in the previous section where the demographic shift was met with a technological change, this cultural shift was met with a purchasing option change in the shopping solution of the department store.

Mr. Selfridge, a retail tycoon from America, identified that in the British market there was no model equivalent to the American department store. His flagship shore, Selfridges on Oxford Street, offered product on display, public washrooms for women, cosmetics and perfume, in-store restaurants, and fashion shows. Selfridges made shopping an entertaining experience—instead of a chore.[51] Mr. Selfridge's success was driven by his relentless and innovative marketing which has become the standard for modern department stores ever since. By being aware of his surroundings and the absence of this specific retail option in his current environment, he took the opportunity to develop what would become one of the most significant retail empires in the world.[52]

One of the aspects of this shopping cultural change was the drive for the instant gratification of an immediate purchase. Prior to the era of the department store, a wealthy person would have to wait several days for their dressmaker to complete their selection and a low-income earner would have to take several days to make their garment. These two individuals could now walk into a store such as Selfridge's and within less than an hour select and purchase the garment of their choice, have it wrapped, and take it home.

In today's environment, we see a similar shift with airline travel. In the past, travellers would sit with a travel agent to discuss their travel options. The agent would contact the airlines and determine the best deal and schedule, print out the multi-form ticket, tuck it into an envelope-sized folder, and offer it to the traveller. Today, travellers peruse their favourite travel websites and within minutes compare fares and schedules, pay with a credit card, and print off their receipt and itinerary. They later download their boarding pass to their mobile device or print it out from the airline website.

In the past, on the day of the flight, travellers would arrive at the airport and stand in line for a service agent who would process their ticket, verify their identification, tag and retain their luggage. Today, travellers go to the airport, approach a kiosk where they print their boarding pass, print their luggage tags, attach their luggage tags to their luggage, and lug their bags over to the bag drop counter.

The common point in the airline and Selfridge examples above is our move to self-service where the customer takes on tasks previously done by others.

Businesses engaged in the travel and retail industries that recognized these coming changes may have taken action. Consider the case of Selfridge's during the time of *Downton Abbey*. This department store would have put tailors and dressmakers out of business unless they could see and adjust to a different business model. A dressmaker would have been smart to focus on wedding gowns or one-of-kind design items to have weathered the industry shift. In the case of travel agents, the ones surviving today have shifted to a specialty product such as tours or cruises or a specialty client base.

Leaders can reduce the risk of being blindsided by external forces that dramatically impact their businesses by being vigilant — minding their surroundings.

1. What political/regulatory changes may be down the road that could impact the organization and industry?

2. What economic changes are on the horizon that may change how the business is run?

3. What demographic changes in society and in the workforce pool may alter how the business is run?

4. What future cultural/societal changes may affect business direction and decisions?

Only if organizations are aware of what may impact their business in the future, can they take responsibility and choose to proactively respond.

*"You are a good spokesman
for Matthew's vision.
Better than he has been."*

Lord Grantham

Chapter Twelve

Sell the Change

(Awareness — Responsibility — *Choice*)

Prior to Lord Grantham's success in the estate's new business model, he struggled with the idea of change. On occasion he was overwhelmed by the new post-war world and all that it meant for his organization and the people who depended on it.

He was also feeling pressure from his new business partner, Matthew Crawley, to make changes. Matthew—confident in his vision— had tried on several occasions to sell his plan to Lord Grantham. Frustrated by Lord Grantham's unwillingness to get on board and support the change, he employed the support of Mr. Murray, Tom Branson, Lady Mary, and Lady Grantham. In the end, it was not Matthew who convinced Lord Grantham to move forward, but rather it was Tom Branson articulating the case in a way that Lord Grantham could accept.

Like Lord Grantham, we know that we must deal with change when it is thrust upon us. But what about initiating change and selling the pace and scope of change to others in our organization? For most leaders, the phrase, "If it isn't broke, don't fix it!" is a way to avoid change, or at least change that is moving at a pace that is uncomfortable.

In the *Downton Abbey* example, clues as to the way each of the management team thinks about the change can be found in the language and metaphors they use. The appropriate pace and scope of the change is different for each of them, leading to heated words, inflated emotions, and defensiveness. As each member attempts to steer the others to their way of thinking, they waste time and energy.

Consider the four characters and their words regarding the change:

Lord Grantham: *"But why not tackle it gradually? Perhaps buy some time by investing your capital."* (54)

- He wants to see incremental change, to fine tune the existing changes, and even avoid new changes if he can.

Lady Grantham: *"But isn't the most important thing, for them or us, to maintain Downton as a source of employment?"* (55)

- She is concerned about the relationships involved in the team. She sees her role is to encourage the others to move forward as a whole.

Tom Branson: *"The estate can offer proper compensation to the tenants now. While the money's there, but if we miss this chance it may not come again."* (56)

- He is attempting to move the organization from one place to another—from tenant farming to offering the farmers an option to sell now.

Matthew Crawley: *"It makes no sense to retain this big of a separate section. No sense at all. But of course Jarvis won't see that because he hates change."* (57)

- He is excited about the change and sees the endless possibilities. He is frustrated by anyone who doesn't embrace the pace and scope of his vision and derides those who resist change.

Each of these characters demonstrates a different metaphor while processing and communicating change.

Consider these four change metaphors: (58)

Fix and Maintain — can be characterized as a ***repair person*** who believes that something has been broken so let's fix it quickly and move on. In the past, Lord Grantham quickly found answers to his problems and just as quickly forgot about them. When he was in financial trouble as a younger man, he married an heiress and then ceased to be overly concerned about the running of his business. Now, again under financial pressure, he wants his partner to invest in the business with further resources and then things will just go back to normal. When the other members of his team push for a more in-depth change, he pushes back.

Build and Develop — can be characterized as the *coach* who believes that if we all just pull together, we can get this done. We can do better than we have in the past; we have a strong foundation to build on. Lady Grantham's goal is to ensure that the team members work together and this change initiative does not cause relationship breakdown. She subtly and quietly points everyone in the right direction so they can move from their different positions and come together in a joint effort.

Move and Relocate — can be characterized as the *planner* who moves the organization from one place to another, not unlike a realtor moving a homeowner from one city to the next. Tom calmly attempts to bring Matthew down from his expansive plans and pull Lord Grantham along at a quicker pace and scope. He believes that they must move from the old, familiar system to a new modern operation.

Liberate and Recreate — can be characterized as a *visionary* who dreams of a brave, new world. Matthew sees change as an opportunity to rethink the business. He believes the past must be abandoned and a new kind of organization created. His focus is on getting to the essence of the business and breaking away from old ways of thinking and performing.

In the *Downton Abbey* example, was Matthew moving too quickly? Is Lord Grantham dragging his heels? Is Branson too transactional and focused on detail? Is Lady Grantham patronizing the team members for the sake of harmony? In any change initiative, some players will think things are moving too fast and others too slow. Some players will believe the changes are too small and others too large.

By listening carefully to how others communicate about change, leaders can decipher the individual's metaphor. The leader can sell the change more effectively once each person's metaphor for change is known and communication is tailored.

"She would be willing the changes to fail."

Dr. Clarkson

Chapter Thirteen

Do No Harm

(Awareness — *Responsibility* — **Choice)**

he Dowager Countess of Grantham was the long-standing president of the Downton Village Hospital. She had been its "doughty champion"[60] for many decades and as a result was very emotionally invested in her vision for the organization.

The sweeping societal changes at the time of *Downton Abbey* included a centralization of healthcare services in Britain. This meant an amalgamation of the Royal York and the Downton Village hospitals.

Like the best champions, the Dowager used every tool in her arsenal to win the day. She lobbied support; called board meetings to influence the stakeholders—and even used a personal relationship to arrange a dinner with the Minister of Health. The Dowager was righteous in her view that keeping control of the hospital would ensure the needs of local citizens would not be lost in ballooning bureaucracy. Her case, however, was defeated in favour of the benefits of shared technology and budgetary savings. After several decades in the role of hospital president, the Dowager Countess was replaced by her daughter-in-law, Lady Grantham.

The Dowager, normally the quintessential example of grace and diplomacy, did not take her loss of control with dignity. She engaged in several arguments at dinner parties and had a very public scene with Lady Grantham in the great hall of the Abbey during the hospital's fundraiser. The Dowager was removed as president as a result of her inability to support the change.

The Dowager's choice to leave or remain was taken from her. Her ability to retire with dignity from the role was lost because she could not see the extent to which her emotions and lack of humility affected her response to the change.

Not only was she wrought with anxiety and angst throughout the change process, but her negativity put a damper on the enthusiasm of others and caused relational strife within the organization and her family.

As discussed earlier in Chapter Three, the Dowager's response to change was the role of the *Obstructionist*—a person who deliberately refuses to support or implement the change because they assume they know better than the legitimate authority in charge.

When managing a change process, it is very important to be part of the solution and not part of the problem — to be moving forward and not dragging the process backward. Leaders may experience changes they cannot support, whether due to a conflict or in principle. Effective change management means knowing when it is time to leave and doing so with as little harm as possible.

How to know when it is time to leave:
1. Are you bored with the change/challenge?
2. Are you finding yourself impatient with coworkers?
3. Do you find yourself defending the old way of doing things?
4. Are you avoiding meetings?
5. Do you feel increased conflict?
6. Are you suffering from increased mental or physical fatigue?

How to leave and do no harm:
1. Make sure the organization has a succession plan for your role—either an interim or permanent replacement.

2. Clarify expectations regarding the transition process with stakeholders and coworkers above and below you to establish both your comfort level and theirs.

3. Accept that not everything will be wrapped up neatly, despite your best efforts.

4. Work as a team with coworkers and stakeholders for onboarding your replacement.

5. Once your replacement arrives, get out of the way, vacate the office, let go, and move on.

A leader puts herself in a tenuous position if she attempts to champion a change she does not support. A good leader will take responsibility and make the choice to leave to ensure the ongoing health of the organization.

"*Mr. Branson is just nervous
that his Lordship
will retreat to his old ways
and abandon all
Mr. Matthew's reforms.*"

Lady Mary Crawley

Chapter Fourteen

Make It Stick

When Matthew Crawley, Lord Grantham's partner, died suddenly in a car crash, Lord Grantham was faced with having to pay the death duties. He decided to use the capital earmarked for the re-engineering plan of the estate. This would put a stop to the move from a tenant-based land rental system to intensive farming. Tom Branson, the Agent at Downton Abbey, was working with Lord Grantham following Matthew Crawley's death to manage the affairs of the estate. Because Lady Mary was George's mother and guardian—and the child was heir to the estate—Tom was interested in hearing Lady Mary's opinion on the payment of the death duties and the path moving forward.

Lady Mary had retreated into her grief. She did not believe she was equipped to assume Matthew's leadership role as change agent for the estate. Finally, she was challenged by Mr. Carson, a senior manager and confidant, to stand up and take on the mantle of leadership. She moved forward into the role to push through Matthew's vision, not allowing his plans to fall by the wayside under Lord Grantham's leadership. If Lady Mary had refused to step up and fill her husband's vacant role as change agent, the new plan would have been condemned to failure.

Like most change initiatives, Downton Abbey's re-engineering plan faced critical moments of potential derailment which would have caused them to become an organization among the many that fail.

First, they lost the champion and the visionary of the change. Secondly, the resources to fund the change seemed in peril or unavailable. Thirdly, the remaining executive members had secondary gain in retaining the status quo.

When organizational change fails, it is often due to one of these three factors:

1. *Power of the champion*

Often organizations have one of their charismatic and well supported leaders kick off change initiatives because they need to get everyone on board and in support of the change. But often these same high performing executives have multiple responsibilities in the organization and are pulled off the change initiative to take on other duties or start new projects.

Whether you lose your champion due to them leaving the organization, being pulled onto other projects, or (in the rare and tragic case of Matthew Crawley in the Downton Abbey example above) die, the organization's change initiative is at great risk of losing its momentum and final success because the champion is not available from beginning to end.

To get through the tough points of change, employees must believe in the change and its goals, be nurtured through the complete process with frequent updates regarding the initiative, receive assurance that the actions they are taking so far are on target and will meet the final goal, and be encouraged by the champion with positive, personal messaging.

2. *Appropriate and available resources*

Many businesses frequently run over budget on change initiatives because—even with the best budgeting process—leaders are attempting to budget the unknown. As a result, most change management budgets will have a degree of margin built in to cover overrun of expenses.

What occurred in the case of Downton Abbey was not a mere 10% over-budget expenditure. The death tax owed by the estate to the Government of Great Britain gutted Matthew Crawley's previous capital investment in the organization.

Although change initiatives may have executive and stakeholder support, they still may be derailed by unknown or unforeseen demands on economic resources and cash flow from another direction.

In the case above, Lady Mary's and Lord Grantham's choices were to abandon the change, put it on hold, or find the money. Mary, after consulting with her friend Lord Gillingham, negotiated arrangements to pay the death tax in installments rather than selling off land. Lady Mary made the deal to keep the land intact and the cash in hand to purchase the leases back from the tenant farmers.

3. *Secondary Gain*

Secondary gain is defined as "the emotional, physical or financial benefit derived from the failure of a course of action".

Although Lord Grantham would be the logical replacement as change champion after the death of Matthew Crawley, he struggled with his conflicting desires to see the success of the initiative versus the benefits of the failure of the plan. If the change initiative continued as planned, Lord Grantham would be required to share authority with his daughter, Lady Mary. If it failed, he would regain full control of the estate—an appealing prospect. Lord Grantham's secondary gain at the failure of the re-engineering plan was to return to sole leadership.

A person could be enthusiastic and believe they are genuinely supportive of a change—yet at an unconscious level perceive economic or emotional challenges which they would rather not face.

Consider these questions a person many ask themselves to explore their secondary gain:

1. If the change is successful, what uncomfortable conversations might I be required to have? Who will I have to fire? Demote?

2. What degree of control will I lose? How much freedom will I lose?

3. What will I now be held accountable for? Will it affect my rating of success, my reputation, or my pay?

4. Who must I report to? Who will no longer report to me?

5. What mental or physical energy will this change demand that may affect my health, my relationships, or my other work obligations?

Secondary gain often exists at an emotional or unconscious level. The communication and behavior that accompanies efforts to actualize the secondary gain can be destructive—personally and professionally. It is essential to know your true motivation in order to protect both your reputation and your relationships.

"Sic transit gloria mundi."

Lady Edith Crawley

A latin phrase that reminds us
all things pass away,
all things change.

Conclusion

n the final season of *Downton Abbey*, Lord Grantham, Lady Grantham, Lady Mary, and Lady Edith attend the estate sale of their close neighbor, Sir John Darnley of Mallerton. In a moment of confession, Sir John comments, *"This life is over for us. It won't come back. We hung on for far too long and now there is nothing left. Learn from us."* (63)

Lord and Lady Darnley were selling off the land and the majority of their possessions, keeping only enough items to fill a much smaller house in London. In a desire to have some sort of successful financial future, their only son, Tim, was emigrating to Kenya at the far reach of the British Empire.

In contrast, Downton Abbey was a hopeful and unique example of an agricultural estate in Britain that survived the sad tragedy of the political will of the day which had buried the majority of similar agricultural estates.

Leaders in today's organizations can learn much from the example of Downton Abbey in managing change, both personally and at a corporate level. Although today's technology and savvy workforce gives us an edge up on managing change, our flattened organizations with minimum structure and confusing reporting systems often leave employees in a place of constant insecurity and anxiety. Never before has it been more necessary to have effective tools to manage change personally and organizationally.

How do we ensure that change initiatives succeed?

The key components to successfully managing change are having awareness, taking responsibility and making choices.

Awareness: We must be aware of what is happening in our organization, industry, society, and culture so we may anticipate change and navigate it well.

Responsibility: We must take responsibility for our attitudes, emotions and actions—both positive and negative.

Choice: We must be proactive in acquiring all the necessary information and then make a choice.

To successfully manage change, an individual may need to change who they are, confront their fears, and act courageously.

When discussing the dramatic changes facing estates like Downton, Lord Grantham and his American mother-in-law, Martha Levinson, summed it up over a glass whisky:[64]

"Sometimes I feel like a creature in the wilds,
whose natural habitat is gradually being destroyed".
Lord Grantham

"But some animals adapt to new surroundings.
Seems a better choice than extinction."
Mrs. Levinson

Notes and References

Introduction

1. "From years of study, I estimate today more than 70% of needed change either fails to be launched, even though some people clearly see the need, fails to be completed even though some people exhaust themselves trying, or finishes over budget, late and with initial aspirations unmet." *A Sense of Urgency* (2008). Written by John Kotter

Chapter One

2. Opening Quote: "I find the whole idea a kind of thief of life. That people should waste hours huddled around a wooden box, listening to someone talking at them, burbling inanities from somewhere else." (Downton Abbey, The Television Series, Season 5, Episode 2)

3. Downton Abbey, The Television Series, Season 5, Episode 2

4. Downton Abbey, The Television Series, Season 5, Episode 2

5. Social Networking Sites, or SNSs, are virtual communities where users can create individual public profiles, interact with real-life friends, and meet other people based on shared interests. In 2004, the most successful current SNS, Facebook, was established and currently has more than 500 million users, of whom 50% log on to it every single day. *The Nielsen Company.* Global Faces and Networked Places (2009)

6. *Internet addiction: Evaluation and Treatment*, Student British Medical Journal (1999) Written by K. Young, Pages 7:351-352

7. "Exploration of Adolescents' Internet Addiction", *Journal of Educational and Developmental Psychology* (2010). Written by L. Li

Chapter Two

8. Opening Quote: "A telephone is not a toy, but a useful and valuable tool". *Downton Abbey — The Complete Scripts — Season 1* (2009). Written by Julian Fellowes, Page 380

9. *Downton Abbey — The Complete Scripts — Season 1* (2009). Written by Julian Fellowes, Page 359

10. Downton Abbey, The Television Series, Season 6, Episode 4

Chapter Three

11. Opening Quote: "But Daisy mustn't find out that I don't know how to work it ... because it makes her part of the future and leaves me stuck in the past." (Downton Abbey, The Television Series, Season 4, Episode 1)

12. Downton Abbey, The Television Series, Season 4, Episode 1

13. Douglas Adams, *Salmon of Doubt* (2002). Adams was an English author, scriptwriter, essayist, humourist, satirist and dramatist. He is known for his book series, *The Hitchhiker's Guide to the Galaxy*, which originated in 1978 as a BBC radio comedy before developing into a series of books that sold more than 15 million copies in his lifetime alone. The posthumously published collection of his latest work, *The Salmon of Doubt*, included an unfinished novel and was published in 2002.

14. *Personal Strategies for Managing Change (1999).* Prepared for Saskatchewan Social Services, Written by Laurelie Martinson

Chapter Four

15. Opening Quote: "You have to set the number on the dial and I had it up too high, but I've got the hang of it now." *Downton Abbey — The Complete Scripts — Season 3* (2014). Written by Julian Fellowes, Page 247

16. *Downton Abbey — The Complete Scripts — Season 3* (2014). Written by Julian Fellowes, Page 224

17. *Downton Abbey — The Complete Scripts — Season 1* (2009). Written by Julian Fellowes, Page 383

18. *Reality Therapy: A New Approach to Psychiatry* (1975). Written by William Glasser, Pages 13-14

19. *General Electric Annual Report* (2000), Page 6

Chapter Five

20. Opening Quote: "Sir Anthony, it must be so hard to meet the challenge of the future, and yet be fair to your employees." *Downton Abbey — The Complete Scripts — Season 1* (2009). Written by Julian Fellowes, Page 273

21. *Downton Abbey — The Complete Scripts — Season 1* (2009). Written by Julian Fellowes, Page 272

22. *Downton Abbey — The Complete Scripts — Season 1* (2009). Written by Julian Fellowes, Page 273

23. *Downton Abbey — The Complete Scripts — Season 1* (2009). Written by Julian Fellowes, Page 273

Chapter Six

24. Opening Quote: "So I told them I will do it, I will drive the tractor." *Downton Abbey — The Complete Scripts — Season 2* (2013). Written by Julian Fellowes, Page 90

25. *Downton Abbey — The Complete Scripts — Season 2* (2013). Written by Julian Fellowes, Page 90

Chapter Seven

26. Opening Quote: "Service is ending for most of us ... there's going to be more and more people chasing fewer and fewer jobs." (Downton Abbey, The Television Series, Season 6, Episode 7)

27. Downton Abbey, The Television Series, Season 6, Episode 7

Chapter Eight

28. Opening Quote: "I've bought a typewriter and I've taken a postal course in shorthand ... Because I want to leave service. I want to be a secretary." *Downton Abbey — The Complete Scripts — Season 1* (2009). Written by Julian Fellowes, Page 141.

29. *Control Theory: A new Explanation of How We Control Our Lives* (1984). Written by William Glasser, Pages 46-47

30. *Downton Abbey — The Complete Scripts — Season 1* (2009), Written by Julian Fellowes, Page 147

Chapter Nine

31. Opening Quote: "Well, I'll rent it out now and then later, I thought I might take in some lodgers." (Downton Abbey, The Television Series, Season 5, Episode 5)

32. This metaphor of using an imaginary hat or cap as a symbol for different thinking areas was first mentioned by Edward De Bono as early as 1971 in his book, *Lateral Thinking for Management*, when describing a brainstorming framework.

33. Downton Abbey, The Television Series, Season 5, Episode 5

34. Downton Abbey, The Television Series, Season 5, Episode 5

35. Downton Abbey, The Television Series, Season 5, Episode 5

36. Downton Abbey, The Television Series, Season 6, Episode 7

37. Downton Abbey, The Television Series, Season 6, Episode 6

Chapter Ten

38. Opening Quote: "Yes, the estate has been run very wastefully." *Downton Abbey — The Complete Scripts — Season 3* (2009). Written by Julian Fellowes, Page 391

39. *Downton Abbey — The Complete Scripts — Season 3* (2009). Written by Julian Fellowes, Pages 391-2

40. "What Makes Great Boards Great", *Harvard Business Review* (September 2002). Written by Jeffrey A. Sonnenfeld, Page 111

41. The Board as a Monitor of Organizational Activity: The Applicability of Agency Threory to Nonprofit Boards. *Nonprofit Management & Leadership* (Volume 12, No. 4, Summer 2002). Written by Judith L. Miller, Page 438

Chapter Eleven

42. Opening Quote: "The wage bill is three times what it was before the war. Soon, it will be worse." (Downton Abbey, The Television Series, Season 6, Episode 1)

43. Downton Abbey, The Television Series, Season 6, Episode 1

44. *Abstract of British Historical Statistics*, 1988. Annual Reports of the Registrar General and Returns of Judicial Statistics, England and Wales, (Wealth and Inheritance in Britain from 1896 to the Present). Written by Mitchell and Deane, Pages 29-30

45. *Rosebery: Statesman in Turmoil, John Murray* (2005). Written by Leo McKinstry, Pages 504-505

46. *Eighty-Second Report of the Commissioners of HM's Inland Revenue for the year ended 31 March 1939*, Page 13 and 95th *Report of the Commissioners of HM's Inland Revenue for the year ended 31 March, 1952*, Page 161

47. According to British accountants: for 2018, the federal estate tax exclusion amount is $5,600,000 per person. Estates that exceed the exclusion amount are subject to a death tax rate of 40%.

48. *Historical Timeline: Farm Machinery and Technology*, https://www.agclassroom.org/gan/timeline/farm_tech.htm, 2014.

49. *Economic History of Tractors in the United States* (2008). Written by William White The tractor has had a markedly positive economic impact. Horses and mules, while providing farm power, ate up more than twenty percent of the food they helped farmers grow. By replacing them with machines that consumed much less expensive quantities of fuel, oil, and hydraulic fluid, farmers were able to reduce their costs and pass these social savings along to food buyers. More importantly, the millions of farm workers freed up by the technology were able to contribute their labor elsewhere in the economy, creating large economic benefits."

50. *How Focus On Technology Can Drive Sales for McDonalds*, https://www.forbes.com/sites/greatspeculations/2017/06/27/how-focus-on-technology-can-drive-sales-for-mcdonalds/#743aa60d434b

51. *Shopping, Seduction & Mr. Selfridge* (2013). Written by Lindy Woodhead

52. *Mr. Selfridge's Romance of Commerce* (2013). Written by Harry Gordon Selfridge.

Chapter Twelve

53. Opening Quote: "You are a better spokesman for Matthew's vision. Better than he has been." *Downton Abbey — The Complete Scripts — Season 3*. Written by Julian Fellowes, Page 460

54. *Downton Abbey — The Complete Scripts — Season 3*. Written by Julian Fellowes, Page 452

55. *Downton Abbey — The Complete Scripts — Season 3*. Written by Julian Fellowes, Page 453

56. *Downton Abbey — The Complete Scripts — Season 3*. Written by Julian Fellowes, Page 388

57. *Downton Abbey — The Complete Scripts — Season 3*. Written by Julian Fellowes, Page 387

58. *Managing the Metaphors of Change*, Organizational Dynamics (Volume 22, Issue 1, Summer 1993). Written by Robert J. Mashak, Pages 44-56.

Chapter Thirteen

59. Opening Quote: "She would be willing the changes to fail." (Downton Abbey, The Television Series, Season 6, Episode 6)

60. *Downton Abbey — The Complete Scripts — Season 1* (2009). Written by Julian Fellowes, Page 131

Chapter Fourteen

61. Opening Quote: "Mr. Branson is just nervous that his lordship will retreat to his old ways and abandon all Mr. Matthew's reforms." (Downton Abbey, The Television Series, Season 4, Episode 1)

Conclusion

62. Opening Quote: "Sic transit gloria mundi." (Downton Abbey, The Television Series, Season 6, Episode 1)

63. Downton Abbey, The Television Series, Season 6, Episode 1

64. *Downton Abbey — The Complete Scripts — Season 3* (2014). Written by Julian Fellowes, Page 135

Acknowledgements

We thank our great team of editors:
Malcolm Bucholtz, Pamela Burns,
Margo Davidson-Wood, Pat Dell,
Carol Fiedelleck, I.J. McIntyre, Carolyn Schur,
and Carole Stepenoff.
They read our first draft
and provided valuable feedback
which has much improved this book.

We thank Julian Fellowes for his
brilliant characters, eloquent dialogue,
and masterful storytelling.

We thank Alastair Bruce, who's expertise
elevated the television series from
a period drama to a historical account.

Looking for more
Lessons From Downton Abbey?

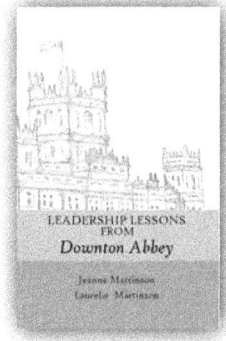

LEADERSHIP LESSONS
FROM
Downton Abbey

Jeanne Martinson
Laurelo Martinson

Leadership Lessons
From Downton Abbey

Section One: Leading Yourself

Discerning Motivation — *"It will be a huge wrench for me to leave Downton."*
Humble Honesty — *"In my vanity and pride, I gave him what he wanted."*
Career Fluidity — *"I am having my career backwards."*
Protecting Legacy — *"If there are changes that need to be made,
we mustn't be afraid to face them."*
Practicing Generosity — *"I don't care for a lack of generosity."*

Section Two: Leading Employees

Defined Roles — *"If I came, they wouldn't have fun .... I'm their leader."*
Strengthening Mentorship — *"Mr. Carson has been a kind and wonderful
teacher."*
Direct Communication — *"It's not nothing, is it?"*
Direct Feedback — *"I hear you are becoming mighty imperious in your manner
with the staff here."*
Maintaining Accountability — *"Has someone forgotten to pay your wages?"*
Taking Action — *"There are rules to this life ....
and if you're not prepared to live by them, then it's not the right life for you."*

Section Three: Leading Culture

Protecting Brand — *"A good servant at all times retains a sense of pride and dignity."*

Respecting Leadership — *"You will therefore please accord him the respect he is entitled to."*

Perceiving Influence — *"Everyone knows you can wrap him around your little finger."*

Professional Relationships — *"Well I can't see that lasting long."*

Marshalling Team — *"We'll all pull together and it'll be great fun."*

Section Four: Leading with Others

Respecting Boundaries — *"I'm not sure that you're entitled to dress down Mrs. Patmore in this way."*

Common Purpose — *"I just want what's best for the village."* *"At least we have that in common."*

Allowing Support — *"I could almost manage ... I don't need a doctor to tell me I'm going blind."*

Intentional Partnering — *"If we each do what we can do, then Downton has a real chance."*

Facebook: Lessons from Downton Abbey

Email: *LessonsFromDowntonAbbey@sasktel.net*

Publisher: WoodDragonBooks.com

Looking for more
Lessons From Downton Abbey?

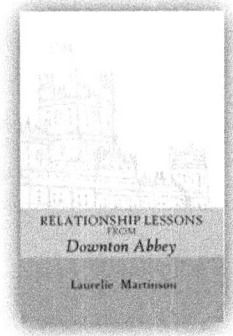

Relationship Lessons
From Downton Abbey

Section One: Loving Spouses

Loving Long — *"Marriage is a long business."*
Loving Complements — *"We were a marriage of equals."*
Loving Exclusively — *"You let him into your private life."*
Loving Honestly — *"Would you have married me in a lie?"*

Section Two: Loving Parents

Loving Fairly — *"I love my children equally."*
Loving Courageously — *"There is more than one kind of good mother."*
Loving Spaces — *"I have decided to go away ...
and return when I have gained control of my tongue."*
Loving Intercession — *"Somehow we must find Edith and we must hear
from her what she wants."*

Section Three: Loving Friends

Faithful Friendship — *"Now that you've accepted him, You'll hear no argument from me."*
Gracious Friendship — *"You saved me from making a fool of myself."*
Dedicated Friendship — *"We must stick together. Your dream is my dream now."*
Resilient Friendship — *"I need to be sure we can disagree without there being any bad feeling between us."*

Section Four: Loving Siblings

Granting Freedom — *"Make the right choice for you and not for us."*
Abiding Loyalty — *"Then be on my side!"*
Reliable Forgiveness — *"I assumed you would be fairly sorry unless you're actually insane."*
Loving Longest — *"Because in the end, you're my sister."*

Facebook: Lessons from Downton Abbey

Email: *LessonsFromDowntonAbbey@sasktel.net*

Publisher: WoodDragonBooks.com

Jeanne Martinson

eanne Martinson is a professional speaker, trainer and best-selling author who has worked internationally and throughout Canada. Since co-founding her own firm, MARTRAIN Corporate and Personal Development in 1993, Jeanne has inspired thousands of participants in her keynote presentations and workshops with her humour, insight and real-world examples.

Jeanne completed her Master of Arts degree in Leadership at Royal Roads University in Victoria, British Columbia, Canada. (Her graduate research focused on the differences and similarities of criminal gang leaders and corporate leaders). Jeanne also holds a Certificate in Organizational Behaviour from Heriot-Watt University (Edinburgh, Scotland) and is certified as a practitioner of NLP (Neuro Linguistic Programming).

Jeanne delivers workshops and keynote addresses to government, associations and the private sector. Her most popular topics are leadership and diversity. As a Canadian bestselling author and strategist in workplace diversity, Jeanne's goal is to assist leaders in understanding diversity issues so they may attract, retain and engage their ideal workforce.

Jeanne takes a leading role in her community, a dedication that was recognized with the Canada 125 Medal, the YWCA Women of Distinction Award, the Centennial Leadership Award (for outstanding contribution to the Province of Saskatchewan), the Athena Award, and the EMCY (the national Diversity award of Canada).

Jeanne has eleven books in print, including:

From Away — Immigration to Effective Workplace Integration which explores the differences between Eastern and Western business mindsets and how those differences affect hiring, leading, and retaining new employees who are immigrants from Asia.

Generation Y and the New Ethic gives concrete information about the different generations found in the workplace today with a focus on work ethic and the motivations and values of Generation Y.

Escape from Oz — Leadership for The 21st Century explores the parallels of the characters in the fable *The Wonderful Wizard of Oz* and our own beliefs about personal and professional leadership.

War & Peace in the Workplace — Diversity, Conflict, Understanding, Reconciliation explores how workplaces are becoming more diverse, how diversity may trigger conflict, and how we can prevent diversity-based conflict from spiraling down into dysfunction.

Tossing the Tiara: Keys to Creating Powerful Women Leaders includes an update on the research from Jeanne's first book, *Lies and Fairy Tales That Deny Women Happiness,* and adds information on gender gap, the impact of news media, and the continuing influence of the Disney princess phenomenon.

Hemingway or Twain? Unleashing Your Author Personality is a book to help non-fiction book authors get their book completed with less stress, time and money.

Contact Jeanne at

Email: **watertiger@sasktel.net**

Telephone: 1.306.59.7993

www.martrain.org

Laurelie Martinson

aurelie Martinson is a communication and behaviour specialist with 25 years of experience working with business, government and community organizations. During her years working as a consultant and teaching management communications at the University of Regina, she continued to coach leaders and employees in the discipline of maintaining personal well-being in the wake of organizational change. Her provocative programs carve a pathway for leaders and employees to improve communication in both hostile and well-functioning environments.

Laurelie developed a model of *Generational Addiction and Dependency* that was used as core training for Saskatchewan Social Services. After years of leading group therapy sessions on issues surrounding codependency, recovery, and spiritual development, Laurelie continues to challenge her clients to accept the consequences of their choices, communication and behaviour—and take the necessary steps to rebuild relationships on the foundations of truth, accountability, and compassion.

Laurelie studied at the University of Saskatchewan and is continuing graduate studies in Ministry Leadership and Counseling at Alberta Bible College.

Contact Laurelie at

Email: wisewords@sasktel.net

YouTube: Wise Words

Facebook: Schooling Fish

Lessons from *Downton Abbey*
Book Series

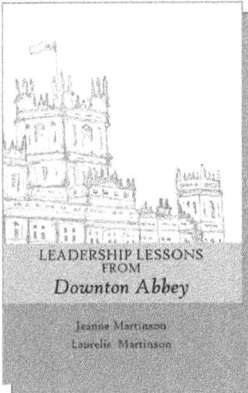

Downton Abbey is an iconic British television series that captivated the world with its portrayal of the transition of family, society and organizational life during the years immediately before and after WWI.

Not only did it sweep away its viewers with dramatic characters, eye catching costumes and cinematography, it provided lessons that can be applied to our world today.

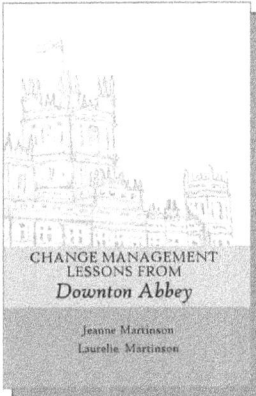

This book series uses illustrations from *Downton Abbey* to communicate timeless wisdom that can improve our personal and professional lives.

Leadership Lessons from
Downton Abbey

Change Management Lessons from
Downton Abbey

Relationship Lessons from
Downton Abbey

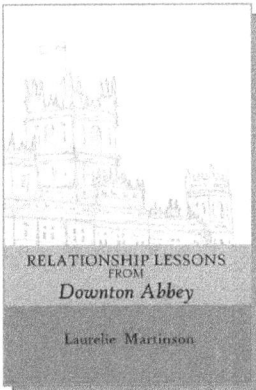

Facebook:
Lessons from Downton Abbey

Email:
LessonsFromDowntonAbbey@sasktel.net

Publisher:
WoodDragonBooks.com

www.ingramcontent.com/pod-product-compliance
Lightning Source LLC
Chambersburg PA
CBHW060612200326
41521CB00007B/753